Magic with Borders

Imagine an instant, stunning border embellishment in a variety of coo___ Die-cuts or stickers become far more hip when placed over a coordinatin___ all repositionable. Even the sticker becomes so when used over the mesh___ Change of mind? No prob-lem. Peel it up and start again. This product allows for foolproof experimenting with no harm to other products.

A Budding Friendship
by Kimberly Sigler

A new friendship is always a good thing. Celebrate with flowers.

MATERIALS: *Magic Mesh* (White large quilt, Red wide weave, Dark Green, Pink, Mauve medium) • Cardstock (Light Blue, Scraps of Lavender, White, Bright Green, Olive Green) • *Emaginations* leaf punch • *Artistic Wire*, 22 gauge wire • Craft glue

INSTRUCTIONS:

Glue a 3½" wide strip of White mesh the entire length on one side of Blue cardstock page. Punch 9 Bright Green and 8 Olive Green leaves. Cut two 2" squares of Red mesh. Take 1 square, hold, diagonal up, and roll slightly from both side corners to create a rosebud. Make 2, set aside. Cut 3 Mauve, 3 Lavender mesh 3" squares. Hold, diagonal up, fold side corners toward center at slightly different angles. Make 6 rosebuds, set aside. Cut eight 1" - 2" squares of Dark Green mesh. Wrap diagonally, around bottom of each rosebud for leaves. Group 1, 2, 2, and 3 buds into bundles. Wrap wire around each grouping, over green mesh, coil the loose end. Arrange rosebuds on White mesh, glue in place. Print 'A Budding Friendship' on White cardstock and mat with Lavender cardstock. Glue punched leaves to White mesh and around words. Make a wire coil 1½" long, glue to word rectangle.

Making Flowers with Mesh

What a clever way to use mesh... create dimensional flowers on a trellis of larger mesh. These are perfect for scrapbook pages and greeting cards. Or create an entire bouquet of colorful mesh flowers to display on a garden page.

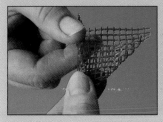

1. Attach medium mesh. Add a layer of large mesh at an angle.

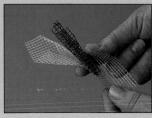

2. Layer and fold flowers.

3. Add wire tendril.

"Cuddlin' with Cocoa"

by Kimberly Sigler

This page will inspire you to grab a cup of cocoa and curl up with the family scrapbook.

MATERIALS: *Magic Mesh* Bronze medium • *Bazzill* cardstock (Red, White, Blue, Brown) • *Ellison* mug die-cut • *Family Treasures* jumbo #3210-16 large snowflake punch • Acid-free adhesive

INSTRUCTIONS:

Cut 1 Red and 1 White strip cardstock 1½" wide x height of page. Cut a 1¼" strip of mesh, adhere to White. Offset White over Red, ¼" Red showing. Glue to Blue cardstock. Attach mug, marshmallows and Brown cocoa to page. Cut swirls from mesh, adhere above cocoa. Punch out snowflakes. Print 'Cuddlin' with Cocoa' on White cardstock. Mat with Red cardstock. Assemble page.

'CUDDLIN' WITH COCOA'

There's No Place Like Home

by Heidi Noll

A little girl in gingham, a perfect page.

MATERIALS: *Magic Mesh* Red medium • Cardstock (White, Red) • *Me and My Big Idea* stickers (1½" flowers, ⅜" alphabet) • Acid-free adhesive

INSTRUCTIONS:

Adhere a 1¼" strip of mesh to left edge of White cardstock. Adhere 3 flower stickers to White cardstock squares; evenly space diagonally over mesh and page. Cut 1 photo round. Mat photos on Red. Arrange rectangles first, then circle slightly overlapping them. With stickers, write 'There's no place like home!' on page around photos.

Lilly Mesh Bound Book

MATERIALS: *Magic Mesh* Black medium • Olive Green watercolor paper • White paper • Paint (Dark Blue metallic, Light Green metallic, Light Blue) • *Art Accents* seed and tube beads (various Blues and Greens) • 10" Metallic Green cord • *Ranger* Product Performers Stickles glitter glue • Acid-free adhesive

INSTRUCTIONS:

Cut, fold and assemble covers according to diagrams. Cut a 1½" x 25⁄16" strip mesh. Lay covers, right side up, ¼" apart. Adhere mesh across both covers and separation. Paint a name and 3 small flowers across bottom 1⅛" of front cover. Glue a stripe of loose beads across cover, between name and mesh. Cut White paper 2¼" x 12" for pages. Accordion fold every 2", starting with center. Slip page ends into covers. Slip cord around mesh spine, make a bow to lay on front cover.

Bind It to Create Texture

Why not decorate and strengthen a book at the same time. Binding altered books or place cards with Magic Mesh is fun and effective. Magic Mesh can easily have a ribbon woven through it to act as a built in bookmark.

Fall Border
by Sarah Cox

This flowing border will set the tone for photos filled with Fall fun.

MATERIALS: *Magic Mesh* Beige wide weave • *It Takes Two* paper (Brown, Ecru) • *EK Success* Fresh Cuts tags with Fall theme • Two ⅛" Gold eyelets • Eyelet setter • Brown pen • 10" Natural jute cord • Brown chalk • Acid-free adhesive
INSTRUCTIONS:
Cut Ecru paper 2¾" wide x height of page. Cut Brown paper 1½" wide. Adhere mesh to Brown paper strip, cut 1 long edge in a wavy pattern. Set eyelets into both tags. Cut jute in half, thread 1 piece through each eyelet, knot loosely. Cut four ⅝" x ⅞" pieces of Ecru paper, lightly color with chalk. Write F, A, L and L on the pieces. Glue Brown mesh strip to Ecru paper strip. Assemble border.

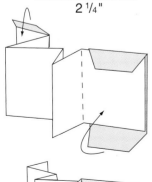

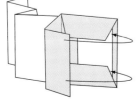

```
      ┌─────────────┐
 4"   │    COVER    │
      └─────────────┘
          2 ¼"
```

DIAGRAM FOR LILLY MESH BOUND BOOK

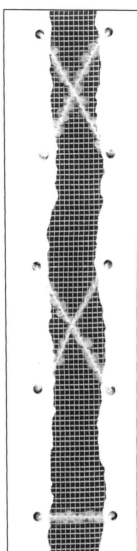

Black and White Laced Border
by Sarah Cox

This spunky border brings to mind tennis shoes and lots of activity.

MATERIALS: *Magic Mesh* White medium • Black cardstock • White embossed cardstock • Ten ⅛" Black eyelets • Eyelet setter • *EK Success* White fibers • Tape • Acid-free adhesive
INSTRUCTIONS:
Cut Black cardstock 3" wide. Adhere mesh to strip, completely covering the Black. Tear 2 pieces of White cardstock approximately 1" wide x height of page along one edge only. One edge will be cut. Glue 1 White strip to each long edge of Black strip. Make sure desired side of embossed White cardstock is showing. Insert 5 evenly spaced eyelets along torn edge. Lace fibers through eyelets, tennis shoe style. Secure ends on back of border with tape or adhesive.

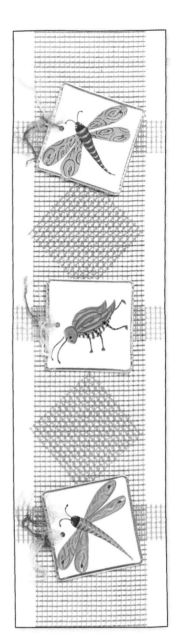

Bugs
by Sarah Cox

These bugs are so colorful you won't care if they are on your side of the screen.

MATERIALS: *Magic Mesh* medium (Plum, Lime Green) • *It Takes Two* White cardstock • *Memories* Three 2" square Metal edged White tags • *Colorbok* bug stickers • *Funky Fibers* 9" Purple/Yellow fibers • Acid-free adhesive
INSTRUCTIONS:
Cut cardstock 3½" wide x height of page. Cut Plum mesh 2½" wide. Adhere to cardstock strip, centering lengthwise. Cut a ¾" wide strip of Lime mesh. Adhere to cardstock horizontally at regular intervals in 3 places. Cut two 1¾" squares of Lime. Adhere diagonally. Stick bugs on tags, make sure bugs are facing desired direction. Thread yarn through tag, knot, leave ends loose. Glue tags to border.

Swim Day with Friends

by Sarah Cox

This border includes a note that compliments the pictures.

MATERIALS: *Magic Mesh* fine (Blue, White) • *SEI* Blue Boardwalk paper • *All My Memories* cardstock (Blue, White) • White Vellum • Four 1½" Silver framed tags • *Graffiti* letter stickers • 4 Blue 3/16" eyelets • Eyelet setter • 10" Blue fibers • Acid-free adhesive

INSTRUCTIONS:

Cover Blue rectangle of Boardwalk paper with Blue mesh. Mat photo on White then Blue. Center and adhere a 2½" wide strip of White mesh over the bottom left Blue square on page. Center 2nd photo in center rectangle at bottom. Adhere a 2½" wide strip of Blue mesh over the Turquoise rectangle. Journal on vellum, and attach to page with eyelets at each corner. Stick S, W, I and M to tags. Thread fiber through holes, careful to keep letters in order. Assemble page. Attach fiber ends to back.

Rub-A-Dub-Dub

by Kimberly Sigler

This would be a great page to show off your little ones playing in the tub.

MATERIALS: *Magic Mesh* (White large quilt, Blue fine) • *Bazzill* cardstock (Gray, Blue, Light Blue, White, Turquoise, Yellow, Dark Yellow) • White vellum • *Family Treasures* punches (circle - ½", ¾", 1", 1¼"; duck - ½", 1¼") • White paint pen • Acid-free adhesive

INSTRUCTIONS:

Adhere 2¾" wide quilt mesh along left side of Gray cardstock, cut top mesh edge at a 45° angle. Cut 3/16" strips of White cardstock, glue over mesh at top. Mat photos on Light Blue, arrange on page. Punch three 1¼" Light Blue card, three 1" Turquoise card, three ¾" vellum and two ½" vellum circles. Arrange on page, add highlights. Layer Blue and Light Blue torn strips of cardstock on White mesh. Adhere a 1¼" strip of Blue mesh to the bottom edge. Punch ducks from 2 Yellow cardstocks. Make a Black dot on ducks for eyes. On White cardstock write 'Rub-A-Dub-Dub'. Cut around words, angling left edge to match mesh angle. Mat on Light Blue. Assemble page.

Little Fish
by Michelle Tardie

Capture your little fish on a great page like this.

MATERIALS: *Magic Mesh* White fine • *Paper Fever* papers (Green plaid, Blue plaid, Blue, Light Blue, White) • *Family Treasures* and *EK Success* circle punches (9/16", 1") • Poem • *Creating Keepsakes* CK Script font • *Internet* Scriptina font • Green fibers • *Emagination* eyelets (17 White 1/8") • Eyelet setter • Three 1½" x 2⅛" Turquoise vellum die-cut fish • Acid-free adhesive

INSTRUCTIONS:
Mat Blue on Green paper. Mat photos on White then Blue. Cut Blue paper 2⅞" x the width of the Blue plaid, cover with White mesh. Glue to bottom of Blue plaid. Cut Light Blue paper 1½" x the width of Blue plaid, cut one long edge in a ripple pattern. Punch three large and three small circles from Blue paper. Punch three large and five small circles from Light Blue. With eyelets, make three circle sets with alternating colors. Glue to rippled strip. Add additional eyelets as bubbles for fish. With ripple edge down, glue to top edge of mesh covered strip. Glue fish under bubbles. Adhere circles between fish. Arrange

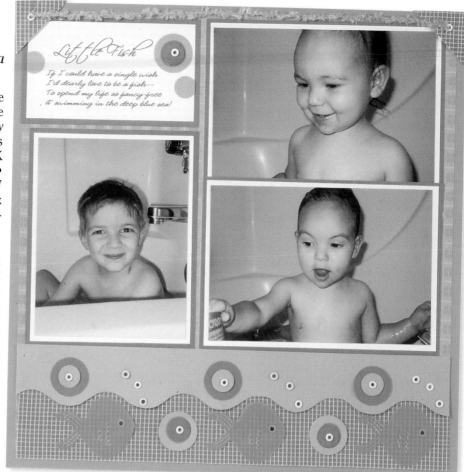

strip and photos on page. Print title and poem on White paper; mat on Blue. Glue to page. Trim 1 edge of two small Light Blue circles. Glue circles to word card. Cut a 1⅜" square of Blue paper, adhere mesh to it. Cut diagonally, glue to top 2 corners, overlapping picture and word card. Insert 1 eyelet in center of each triangle, thread fiber through both. Glue ends to back.

Poolside Fun
by Sarah Cox

Mix sunshine, one swimming pool and a bunch of kids. You have an instant party.

MATERIALS: *Magic Mesh* fine (Orange, Yellow, Green, Blue, Purple) • Turquoise cardstock • *All My Memories* Aqua Time Savers Design 4 paper • Stickers (pastel ¼" dots, 1" round alphabet, 7/16" alphabet) • Acid-free adhesive

INSTRUCTIONS:
Turn Time Savers paper so the large Light Blue rectangle is at the top. Cut one 2⅝" square of Orange, Purple and Green mesh. Adhere to top half of page at random angles. Adhere Yellow mesh to the middle Light Blue rectangle. Cut one 2" square of Orange, Purple, Green and Blue mesh. Adhere one each, from left in the same order, to Light Blue squares at page bottom. Mat 3 photos on cardstock. Glue across large rectangle at top of page. Trim smaller photo to fit within Yellow mesh space, attach. Stick 3 small dots to right of photo. Stick 1 letter in center of each bottom square, spelling 'Pool'. Stick 'SiDE' at an angle on the right.

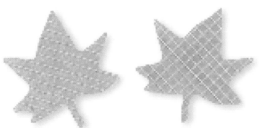

Die-cut Leaves work well in Browns, Reds and Yellows on pages with fall themes. But don't overlook the Greens when designing for spring. These leaves are Deluxe Cuts small maple leaf #3-007. Leaves play a prominent role on pages 22 and 23.

Endless Choices of Die-cuts are available from *Sizzix*, seen here, and other companies. Adhere mesh to your paper before cutting or leave the mesh backing in place, die-cut, then peel the backing off before positioning on your project.

Ice Cream would work with pages of children or adults. The cone here is *Magic Mesh* medium weave while the ice cream is *Magic Mesh's* Dotti Ann. Combining your meshes on the many die-cuts available just adds to the fun. Dotti Ann can be seen on page 27.

This Snowman and Snowflakes are used to great advantage in the tag seen on page 2. *Emagination* has a large selection of winter theme punches, as do many other sources. *Family Treasures* snowflake is used in projects on pages 2 and 4.

Pumpkins, Pumpkins Everywhere with these *Deluxe Cuts* stacked pumpkins, #4-017, are the perfect addition to any page having a fall or Halloween theme. Here the Orange was covered with Yellow Magic Mesh before cutting.

Fishing

by Sarah Cox

Every kid needs to go fishing. Capture the moment with snapshots displayed on this great page.

MATERIALS: *Magic Mesh* Beige wide • *It Takes Two* paper (White, Brown cardstock, 2 Green papers) • Tags (4" x 8"; three 2⅛" x 3½") • Funky Fibers (3½" Brown shaggy, 14" Brown boucle) • Brown feathered fishing lure • *Sizzix Machine* (1½" letters die) • Acid-free adhesive

INSTRUCTIONS:
Cover tags with paper. Apply a 3" wide strip of mesh to a 3¼" x 8" piece of Green paper. Adhere a 2¼" x 7¼" piece of Brown cardstock on mesh. Adhere mesh to additional Brown paper, die-cut 'Fishing'. Adhere. Glue assembly across page bottom. Glue only side and bottom edges to form a pocket. Cut 3 photos to fit on smaller tags, mat on Brown, glue to tags. Cut a photo to fit on larger tag, mat on Brown, glue on tag. Adhere 2⅝" x 4" mesh to end of tag. Cut boucle fiber into 3 equal lengths. Tie 1 to each small tag. Tie shaggy fiber to larger tag. Attach lure to large tag. Slip the 3 smaller tags into pocket, adhere at various angles.

Make Die-Cuts with Mesh

Magic Mesh is easily die-cut to form letters and shapes with dimension. Simply stick down on paper and punch or die-cut. Once you've made your shape you may peel it up from paper to echo a pattern or simply use it in its multi dimensional form straight from the machine.

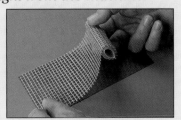

1. Cover cardstock with mesh. Trace shapes or letters with a template. Cut them out.

2. Or use a Sizzix machine to die-cut shapes and letters.

Visit to the Pumpkin Patch
by Cindy Harris

A scarecrow with a smile invites you into his pumpkin patch.

MATERIALS: *Magic Mesh* Beige medium • Cardstock (Rust, Gold wash, Golden) • Pumpkin color Eyelets (⅛", ³⁄₁₆") • Eyelet setter • Rust raffia • Wood cut-outs (pumpkin, scarecrow) • *Sizzix* machine • 1¾" and 2" Alphabet die • Two ⅜" Rust colored buttons • Paper letter tiles • Two 1¼" round tags • Black pen • Pop Dots • Acid-free adhesive

INSTRUCTIONS:
Mat Gold cardstock with Rust. Cut a 6½" x 7¼" piece of Rust, adhere a photo on the left. Adhere mesh to Golden cardstock. Die-cut smaller 'patch' from adhered strip. Die-cut 'patch' from Rust. Glue mesh letters to Rust. Glue a button for the hole in the 'p' and 'a'. On 1 tag write the month, on the other write the year. Thread raffia through each tag, knot with a 2" loop Glue photo rectangle across center of page. Glue 'patch' to page. Hang month tag to the 't'. Mat a Golden shape on Rust. Cut a piece of mesh, adhere at an angle. Glue pumpkin and scarecrow to mesh. Cut a ¾" x ⅞" piece of Gold cardstock. Attach at top of shapes, extending over edge. Punch a hole through all layers, set a ⁵⁄₁₆" eyelet. Glue entire unit to bottom right of page, over part of the Rust rectangle. Tie 2nd tag to raffia tassel, do not trim tassel. Above 'patch' glue letters to spell 'At the'.

A Wheelbarrow Full of Pumpkins
by Cindy Harris

Who can resist fields of bright Orange pumpkins. Create this page in wonderful Fall colors.

MATERIALS: *Magic Mesh* Beige medium • Cardstock (Rust, Gold wash, Golden) • Pumpkin colored eyelets (⅛", ³⁄₁₆") • Eyelet setter • Rust raffia • Wood cut-outs (pumpkins, wagon) • Acid-free adhesive

INSTRUCTIONS:
Mat Gold cardstock with Rust. Mat photo at top of a Rust rectangle, leaving 1¼" at bottom. Wrap bottom with raffia, secure ends on back. Journal on Golden cardstock. Set eyelets in corners. Mat a Golden shape on Rust. Cut a piece of mesh, adhere at an angle. Glue pumpkins, then wagon over mesh. Cut a ¾" x ⅞" piece of Gold cardstock. Attach at top of shapes, extending over edge. Punch a hole through all layers, set a ⁵⁄₁₆" eyelet in hole. Cut 10 - 12 pieces of raffia 5" long, fold and push loop through eyelet. Pull ends through loop for tassel. Glue to page. Trim raffia ends to match top of page. Glue unframed photo to bottom left. Glue framed photo to top right. Photo may overlap. Attach words at bottom right.

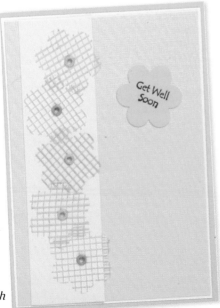

Get Well Soon Card
by Jana L. Millen

Help someone you love feel better with this sweet bunch of flowers gathered just for them.

MATERIALS: *Magic Mesh* fine (Rose, Lavender, Mint Green) • *Bazzill* cardstock (White, Pink, textured Light Yellow) • *All Night Media* flower punch • *Hero Arts* greetings stamp ('Get Well Soon') • *Memories* Black ink • *Doodlebug* eyelets (Lavender, Mint Green, Yellow) • Eyelet setter • Acid-free adhesive

INSTRUCTIONS:
Cut Pink cardstock to desired size, fold to make card. Mat Yellow cardstock on White then card front. Cut a 1⅜" wide strip of White cardstock. Glue to Yellow. Punch 5 flowers from mesh, 2 Rose, 2 Lavender, 1 Green. Adhere flowers to White, staggered and overlapping. Set eyelets in center of flowers, vary the colors. Punch 1 flower from Pink cardstock, stamp 'Get Well Soon' in the center. Glue flower to card.

Homemade Hoops
by Cindy Harris

Throwing a ball through a hoop can keep little ones busy for hours. Lots of photo ops.

MATERIALS: *Magic Mesh* Navy fine • *DMD* cardstock (Dark Blue, Yellow, White) • *Paper Loft* wood pattern paper • *Paper Adventures* Silver metallic paper • 12 Miniature Silver brads • *Provo Craft* 3/8" White alpha stickers • Black fine tip pen • *Scrap Pagerz* lettering template • *DMC* White floss • *Fiskars* crimper • Craft glue

INSTRUCTIONS:

Dark Blue cardstock is your page. Trim Yellow cardstock 1/4" smaller than Blue in height and width, center and glue Yellow onto Blue. Trim wood pattern paper 1/2" smaller than Blue in height and width, center and glue to Yellow. Mat photos with White cardstock; glue on page. Journal on White 3" x 4" and adhere to page. Cut a 2" x 4" rectangle from Yellow cardstock. Cover it with mesh. Cut rectangle into 2 squares, cut each diagonally. Place 1 on each corner of the wood paper. Secure each with 3 miniature brads. Cut metallic paper 3/4" x 3 1/2", crimp. Stick the work 'HOMEMADE' to it near top edge. Punch 5 small holes in paper and sew floss through it, allowing floss to fall in loose loops. Knot on top, trim ends. Adhere mesh to Yellow cardstock. Cut out 'HOOPS'. Cut out a slightly larger Navy 'HOOPS'. Glue Yellow to Navy. Place slightly over right edge of top photo to edge of page borders. Overlap letters a little. Cut 2 ovals and a 'D' shape from Navy paper. Place for center of O's and 'P'.

Polly
by Karan Smith

Kids have always had special times with their pets. A moment like this deserves its own special page.

MATERIALS: *Magic Mesh* medium (Blue, Yellow) • Cardstock (Blue, White, Green, Yellow) • *Sizzix* machine • 1 3/4" Letters die • White vellum • *Funky Fibers* Green/Blue fibers; Feathers (Green, Gray) • *Collage Art* two 3/4" flat glass marbles (opaque Green, clear Green) • Craft glue

INSTRUCTIONS:

White cardstock is your page. Tear a 2 1/2" strip from lower third of Yellow cardstock. Apply Blue mesh on page where strip was torn. Adhere Yellow cardstock over edges of mesh. Cut a 2 3/8" x 4 3/4" piece of White cardstock, adhere Yellow mesh to it. Angle top corners of White with mesh like a tag. Print 'Parker Loves Polly!' on vellum. Tear around the words, glue to Yellow mesh. Cut 6" fiber, fold in half. Glue fold under clear marble at top of Yellow mesh. Trim the photo subject from one photo, glue to Blue mesh. Stretch yarn across Blue mesh area and on top of photo, secure ends on back. Mat photo with Blue, then White cardstock. Glue feathers in a bundle to bottom right corner of larger photo, glue opaque marble to feathers. Adhere Blue mesh to a 2" strip of Green cardstock. Die-cut 'Polly'. Adhere to bottom Yellow strip.

Rubber Stamping on Mesh

Heart in My Hand Art Tag
by Marah Johnson

Tags make perfect little canvasses for the creative. This one is way beyond the identification stage.

MATERIALS: *Magic Mesh* (Red medium, Gold fine) • ½" x 1⅜" White cardstock • 2¾" x 4¾" Corrugated cardboard tag • *All Night Media* alpha stamp, ink pads (Red, Gold) • *Stampendous* (corner stamp, Gold embossing powder) • *Accu-Cut* Baby Hand die-cut • *American Clay* Art-Emboss Gold metal • *Darice* 20 gauge Copper wire • 10 Red E beads • *Funky Fibers* Purple and Orange fibers • *Suze Weinberg* UTEE • Heat gun • Acid-free adhesive

INSTRUCTIONS:
Peel the flat paper from front of tag, adhere Red and Gold mesh. Stamp 'ART' on cardstock, cut out. Stamp a piece of clear plastic with corner stamp and Gold ink. Glue art and corner on tag. Coat 'ART' with UTEE, heat word and corner. Weave wire with beads through wrist. Tie fibers to tag, trim to 5".

HAND PATTERN

Stamp on It

Magic Mesh is wonderful as is, but have you ever thought of stamping it? Increase your design possibilities by creating patterned strips for any occasion. For a textured look take a bold-faced rubber stamp with a simple image. Using permanent ink, stamp mesh on the nonsticky side. Let it dry and stick it to your project.

Tie colors together, emphasize your theme. Simple designs will be easier to recognize because with Magic Mesh most of your surface is holes!

Snuggle Bunny Tag
by Cindy Harris

This sweet little tag would be a cute gift for a child.

MATERIALS: *Magic Mesh* fine weave (assorted pastel colors) • Cardstock tags (3½" x 6½" Pink, 3" x 6" White) • ⅞" x 3½" strip Yellow felt • 3 Pastel flower buttons • Yellow eyelet • Eyelet setter • Yellow thread • Pink chalk • Black pen • Pink die-cut bunny • Foam pads • Purple fibers • Acid-free adhesive

INSTRUCTIONS:
Mat White on Pink tag. Set eyelet. To make a plaid pattern, weave assorted colors of ½" wide mesh strips together. Write motto. Position mesh, felt strip and motto to tag. Sew buttons on felt. Add chalk accents to bunny. Draw details on bunny with pen. Glue to tag, attach face with foam pads. Tie fibers to tag.

This is what happens when you try to ride on your brother's handlebars!

Layer with Mesh!

Magic Mesh can be layered for more variety of looks and added dimension. Create your own plaid to reflect colors used in your project. To mute mesh, cover with a White overlay, to make a color vivid, double or triple it. Try turning mesh at different angles and combining weaves of Magic Mesh, too.

Boo Boo
by Kimberly Sigler

Remember a child's trip to the doctor with a special scrapbook page.

MATERIALS: *Magic Mesh* Creemsicle medium • White cardstock • *Bo Bunny Press* doctor paper • *Create a Cut* 1½" Pink letters • *Accu-Cut* Band-Aid die-cut • Black pen • Acid-free adhesive
INSTRUCTIONS:
Cut two 3" x 8" strips of mesh. Round the corners on one end of each. Adhere to bottom of page overlapping in the middle. Assemble page.

Down n' Dirty
by Kimberly Sigler

Outdoor play provides many opportunities for wonderful memories.

MATERIALS: *Magic Mesh* Brown fine • *Bazzill* cardstock (White, Brown, Tan, Yellow, Green) • *Accu-Cut* die-cut shoe • *Emagination* jumbo splat punch • Black & Gold markers • Acid-free adhesive
INSTRUCTIONS:
Adhere a 2½" wide mesh strip 1½" from bottom. Tear 1 strip each of Tan and Brown. Die-cut shoe and punch splats. Accent shoe with markers. Write 'Down 'n Dirty' on White. Glue to Tan. Assemble page.

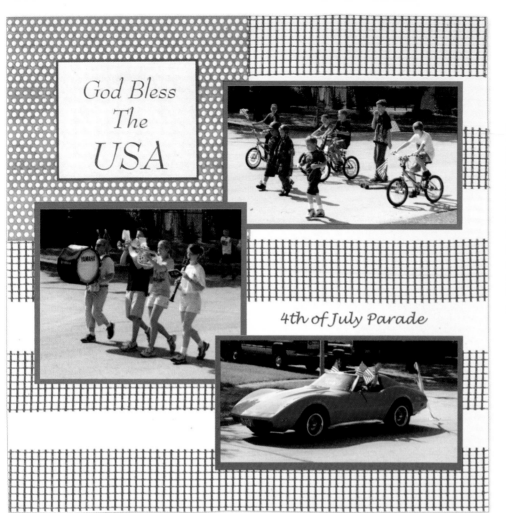

4th of July Parade

God Bless the USA
by Kimberly Sigler

Celebrate freedom with this bright flag page.

MATERIALS: *Magic Mesh* (Red medium, Blue Dotti Ann) • *Bazzill* cardstock (White, Blue) • Black pen • Acid-free adhesive

INSTRUCTIONS:
Cut four 1½" wide strips of Red mesh, cut 1 in half. Cut three 2" x 6" strips of Dotti Ann, adhere to page overlapping to make a 5½" x 6" wide field. Attach Red stripes. Write 'God Bless The USA on White, mat on Blue. Mat photos on Red and Blue.

Loving Snow
by Jeannette Goyke

Save that snow memory to enjoy while you sit by the fire.

MATERIALS: *Magic Mesh* Light Blue fine • *DMD* cardstock (Black, Navy); Vellum • *Colorbok* print paper • *Chatterbox* lettering template • Black pen • *Artistic Wire* 24 gauge Silver • Large snowflake punch • White ink pad • Clear embossing powder • Heat gun • Glitter • Acid-free adhesive

INSTRUCTIONS:
Mat print paper on Black. Cut a 2⅜" wide strip of Black, tear a 2" wide strip of Navy. Stamp all mesh with ink pad, sprinkle with embossing powder mixed with glitter, emboss with heat gun. Punch 3 snowflakes from mesh. Adhere to Navy. Wrap wire around strip. Mat 2 photos on Black. Make photo corners from Navy and mesh. Attach to 3rd photo. Lay mesh over Navy strip. Stamp ink pad through, remove mesh. Heat emboss with powder and glitter. Cut out 'snow' from the strip. Wrap 's' with wire, adhere a piece of mesh under it. Write words on vellum. Assemble page. Adhere small pieces of mesh to vellum, write 'loving' above 'snow'.

Alexander loves to play in the snow, the snow was so deep he mostly just fell which is just fine with him it is all part of the fun.

31 December 2000

loving SNOW

Celebrate Spring
by Michelle Tardie

Beautiful spring days invite the whole family outdoors. Don't forget the camera!

MATERIALS: *Magic Mesh* fine (Pink, Green, White) • *Bazzill* cardstock (Dark Green, Light Green, Pink, White) • *Daisy D's Paper* (gingham Green, Pink) • *My Mind's Eye* stickers (large Green alphabet, Pink frame) • *Paper Fever* small Green alphabet stickers • *Sizzix* machine and dies (tag, fence, dragonfly) • *Karen Foster* White brads • *Craf-T* Pink metallic Rub-Ons • Acid-free adhesive

INSTRUCTIONS:

Mat Green gingham smaller on Dark Green page, mat White on gingham. Mat a photo on Light and Dark Green cardstock. Place frame over photo. Adhere 2½" wide Pink mesh to bottom of White square. Cut waves on 1 long edge of a 1½" wide strip of Green mesh, place over Pink. Make 2 tags from Pink cardstock, insert brads for holes. Stick a piece of White mesh to each. Die-cut 2 dragonflies from Pink gingham. Place on tags. Assemble page. Place words on page with stickers.

Wet n' Wild
by Kimberly Sigler

Let a day at the beach or in the pool inspire you. Go for the Blues.

MATERIALS: *Magic Mesh* fine (Blue, Green, Mint) • *Bazzill* solid cardstock (Turquoise, Blue, Light Blue, Dark Blue) • *Emaginations* jumbo splat punch • Black pen • Acid-free adhesive

INSTRUCTIONS:

Cut 1 strip of Blue and 1 of Mint mesh 2⅜" wide, cut 1 Green 1¼" wide. Adhere to page at an angle. Die-cut splats from Turquoise, Blue and Light Blue. Write words on paper, mat with Blue. Mat photo with Dark Blue. Assemble page.

Collage Away with embellishments!

Wild About the Zoo
by Kimberly Sigler

Lions and tigers and bears! Big or little, everyone loves the zoo.

MATERIALS: *Magic Mesh* fine (Copper, Black) • *Bazzill* cardstock (Tan, Rust, Black, White) • *Making Memories* leopard print paper • Pony beads (Beige, Tan, Brown) • *Artistic Wire* 20 gauge Copper • Black pen • Acid-free adhesive

INSTRUCTIONS:
Tear a 2¼" wide wave edge on a strip of leopard paper, cut a 1½" wide wave edge on another. Adhere a 1¾" strip of Copper mesh on right edge of page. Cut a 2½" wide strip of Copper mesh, cut a 3" wide strip of Black mesh. Thread 18" of wire through long edge of Copper mesh, adding beads, creating loops at intervals. Adhere Black mesh to Copper, leaving 1" beaded edge exposed. Write words on paper, mat on Black. Assemble page.

Long Point Beach
by Sarah Cox

Weave your fiber through each tag as you weave it through the mesh. Adhere all at once.

MATERIALS: *Magic Mesh* Lime medium • *SEI* papers (Barn stripe, Tan, Lime) • *SEI* alphabet stickers (¼", ¾") • *Making Memories* 1" round tags • *Funky Fibers* Brown metallic fibers • Acid-free adhesive

INSTRUCTIONS:
Cut a 3" x 7¼" strip of mesh. Spell name with small letters on tags. Weave yarn through tags and mesh. With 1" letters, spell location along stripes. Mat photo on Lime and Tan. Assemble page.

Love Card
by Jana L. Millen

Make someone feel special with this sweet little love card.

MATERIALS: *Magic Mesh* Lavender fine • *Bazzill* cardstock (White, Pink) • *Pages in a Snap* Lavender paper • *Bucilla* ¼" Pink variegated satin ribbon • *Craft Narrows* ⅝" Lavender ribbon • *Hero Arts* Love rubber stamp • *Making Memories* page pebble • ¼", ½" circle punches • Tapestry needle • Pop Dots • Acid-free adhesive

INSTRUCTIONS:

Cut a 5½" x 8" piece of cardstock, fold to make card. Cover front with Lavender paper. Cut a 2" x 3½" tag from Pink cardstock. Adhere a 2" wide strip of mesh at an angle across tag. With needle, punch a heart shape in center of mesh. Sew Pink ribbon vertically through the holes. Reinforce tag hole, tie Lavender ribbon through tag. Attach Pop Dots then tag to card.

PATTERN FOR HEART

Silly
by Jana L. Millen

Good times with friends. Catch the giggles on film for posterity.

MATERIALS: *Magic Mesh* Pink fine • *Doodlebug Design* paper (stripes, dots, Yellow, Peach, White) • *Making Memories* (⅝", ¾", ⅞" buttons, 1⅞" tag) • *Hero Arts* printers' type alphabet stamps • *Memories* Black ink • Two Orange eyelets • Eyelet setter • *DMC* Yellow embroidery floss • Acid-free adhesive

INSTRUCTIONS:

Cut a 5¾" wide piece of striped paper the direction of the stripes. Adhere to left side of dot paper. Cut a 2⅛" wide strip of mesh. Weave 'Silly' into right half of mesh. Cut a 1¾" circle of Yellow paper, stamp with names. Glue to tag. Set eyelet into tag. Sew on buttons. Glue Peach rectangle to page. Mat photo on Yellow, then White. Set eyelet in bottom left of mat. Attach photo to page. Thread floss through mat and tag eyelets, tie a bow on tag front. Stamp date on page.

Sewing through Mesh

If you're looking for an easy way to attach wire and fibers, try using Magic Mesh. No drying time involved and it adds a dimensional factor to the project. Pick your mesh, sew or weave through it and stick it in place. Even when weaving through just a few strands, it will be solid enough to hold a section of wire. Experiment freely with these sometimes tricky additions. You can easily remove and rearrange them with Magic Mesh.

1. Use a tapestry needle with fibers. Sew or weave through the mesh.

LAURA SAMI CASSIE

JULY 2002

Be With Family
by Jennifer McIntyre

Family pictures don't have to be stiff. Loosen up and enjoy one like this for years to come.

MATERIALS: *Magic Mesh* Tan fine • *DMD* cardstock (Brown, Rust, Red, Blue, Tan) • *Making Memories* (twistel, tag) • *Hillcreek Designs* (buttons, yarn) • *Clipola* spiral clips • *Jolee's Boutique* (buttons, clock) • *Craft-T* chalk • Acid-free adhesive

INSTRUCTIONS:
Mat light Tan cardstock with Red and Brown. Print all text for tags. Cut phrases apart, cut tag shaped. Cut three 2½" x 9" strips of mesh. Adhere to middle of page. Cut a Blue free form mat for photo. Sew some phrases to mesh with buttons, attach 2 to clips. Mat 1 saying with Rust, add clock and tie twistel through tags. Cut title from Rust cardstock. Assemble page.

Discover
by Sarah Cox

Fall is a great time to explore the outdoors. Remember it's colors with this warm page.

MATERIALS: *Magic Mesh* Tan medium • *Cloud 9 Design* paper (Tri-Rip, Finishing Touches) • Acid-free adhesive

INSTRUCTIONS:
Tri-Rip is the page. Cut mesh 1¾" wide, adhere over Rust and Brown junction. Adhere a 1¾" x 3" piece of mesh to lower left of page. Cut frame from Finishing Touches paper. Glue at top left of page. Cut two 1½" x 5⅝" strips of mesh, adhere to top and bottom inside of frame. Attach photo to mesh on frame. Cut word pictures from paper, attach to mesh. Cut paper bundle picture, glue under frame. Mat smaller photo on Brown. Assemble page.

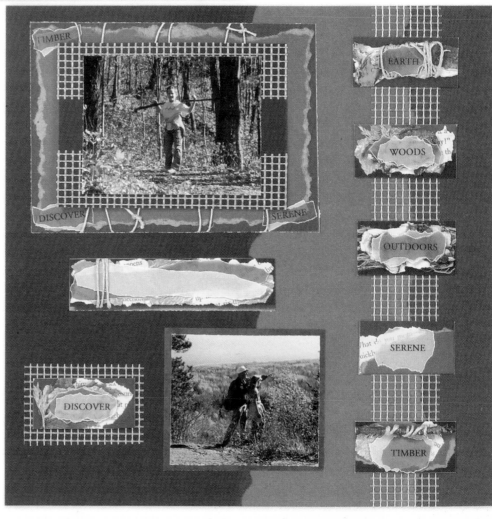

Warmed, Touched and Blessed

by Sarah Cox

Celebrate a special relationship with daisies.

MATERIALS: *Magic Mesh* White fine • *Carolee's Creations* paper (Olive Green, Yellow dot, Summer Daisy Trim) • *Making Memories* buttons • *It Takes Two* poem • *Funky Fibers* variegated fibers • Five 1" daisies with wire stem • Acid-free adhesive

INSTRUCTIONS: Mat photo and 1¾" strip of Olive Green paper on Yellow. Cut mesh to fit on Olive Green. Weave daisy stems through mesh, sewing buttons in place with the wires. Print poem on Olive Green, cut out, punch holes. Thread yarn through holes and large button, knot on top. Assemble page.

you've WARMED ME
with your smile
you've TOUCHED ME
with your love

you've BLESSED ME
with your life

Weaving Flower Stems Through Mesh

Why not let flowers weave their way through your mesh! They do it in nature, always seeking the sun. Bring a little sunshine to your scrapbook with this bright idea.

1. Stick wire stem through mesh.

2. Pull daisy flush with surface.

3. Weave stem through mesh and button.

4. Use stem to secure button to mesh, fold end under.

Sew on it or through it!

You can sew things to Magic Mesh before adhering it to your surface. This is especially helpful when decorating card fronts where you don't want perforations on the inside.

Easter Morn
by Nancy Turnbaugh

Holidays are such fun for kids. Save those smiles with a page fit for the occasion. This clever Easter idea will be just perfect for your little chicks!

MATERIALS: *Magic Mesh* Tan medium • Cardstock (Tan, Yellow, Dark Yellow, Red, White, Black, Brown, Dark Gray, Ecru, Orange, Green) • *Deja View* alphabet • *Frances Meyer* alphabet • *Sizzix* Machine and clouds die • *Accu-Cut* die-cuts (grass and sun) • Black pen • *Magic Scraps* Metallic Yellow grass • *Making Memories* brads(4 Gold; 3 Red) • *Craft T* chalk (Brown, Light Blue) • Rooster, chicken, duck and 2 sizes of egg die cuts • Acid-free adhesive

INSTRUCTIONS: Make an accordion folded egg. For a 2" wide egg, fold 1¾" wide White paper back and forth to desired thickness. Cut paper doll style, smaller than cover of egg. Trim pictures, glue to colored paper, then pages. Add writing if desired. Mat photos to colored paper. Tear Brown and Green paper for grass and dirt, chalk with Brown. Cut Gray and Black paper for chicken coop, adhere to page. Cut Tan rectangle for laying box, cut mesh for chicken wire. Cut 'Easter' in 2 sizes, Gray larger than Tan. Accent Tan letters with pen, glue to Grey. Cut clouds and sun. Chalk Light Blue on clouds. Cut 2 mesh strips 1½" wide, width of the pages. Glue feet to duck, larger chicken and all eggs. Cut three fence posts from Tan cardstock. Draw details on birds, eggs and posts. Cut ⅝" x 1⅝" piece mesh. Assemble elements. Glue grass, Green and Brown strips and adhere mesh to page bottoms. Glue picture pages to egg. Glue Red paper square to chickens. Affix brads to corners of coop mesh. Cut 3 pieces of mesh where 'morn' will be placed. Attach 'morn'. Glue Red triangle brad in center of 'o', Red circle brads to the A and R. Glue 'Easter' in sky.

Make a Mosaic

Create a tile look by adhering Magic Mesh to a piece of paper. Using its grid properties, fill the squares with glue and sprinkle on beads or shaved ice. Lift mesh and you have your mosaic.

Beach'n
by Nancy Turnbaugh

Catching a friend in all her glory is certainly worth a special page.

MATERIALS: *Magic Mesh* Red medium • Cardstock (Brown, Blue, Turquoise, Light Blue, White, Black) • *Paper Bliss* (sandals, tree, coconut drink) • *Sizzix* machine and Alpha die • ½" star punch • Chalk • Red 20 gauge wire • Acid-free adhesive

INSTRUCTIONS:
Tear paper, chalk edges. Layer Brown, Blue and Turquoise on Light Blue paper. Adhere mesh to 1¾" wide Turquoise strip, cut letters. Cut mesh for apostrophe. Attach letters and stars to page. Mat a photo on White and Turquoise. Glue to waves. Assemble and glue sandals, tree and drink to page, attach fruits with wire. Adhere small pieces of mesh to sandals, tree and coconut.

Magic Mesh Overlay

Overlay mesh on die-cuts.

After placing letters or die-cuts, adhere mesh over them. Subtle variations will keep 'em guessing.

Visiting
by Nancy Turnbaugh

A visit with grandparents is something you'll want to remember.

MATERIALS: *Magic Mesh* Purple fine • *Keeping Memories Alive* pattern paper (Berry Blossom, plaid) • Cardstock (Purple, Cranberry, White) • *Making Memories* (8 Gold brads, Silver metal alphas 1⅛" capitals, ¾" lower case) • *EK Success* Purple fibers • Acid-free adhesive

INSTRUCTIONS:
Cut a 2⅜" strip of plaid paper, cut a ¼" strip of Cranberry. Glue Cranberry to bottom third of plaid. Glue plaid to bottom of Berry Blossom. Attach 'Visiting' with brads. Cut a ¼" strip of Purple, cover top of plaid. Cover with a ⅞" strip of mesh, overlapping both edges. Mat small photos on White, then Purple, shape like tags. Tie yarn through each tag, knot. Print journaling around larger photo. Mat large photo on Cranberry, then White. Assemble page.

Leaf Fight *by Kelly Anglin*

A fall outing to the park and the zoo! What could be better?

MATERIALS: *Magic Mesh* Black fine • *DMD* (White, Grey linen cardstock, Yellow vellum) • *Scrap Pagerz* letter template • *Lasting Impressions* leaf template • Silver gel pen • Acid-free adhesive

INSTRUCTIONS:

Create letters and leaves with templates. For 'leaf fight' page, mat 4 photos together on White. Cut a 3" wide piece of mesh, adhere over words on page. Glue small leaf over mesh. With pen, draw the leaf's path, write about the day. For 2nd page, journal on vellum. Tear the word strip and a plain strip. Adhere to lower third of page. Cut two 3" wide pieces of mesh, adhere to top corners of page. Glue leaves on mesh. Mat 2nd page photos separately, place one on a larger mat. Cut notches in 2, place larger photo above notched ones. Assemble page. Cut small squares of mesh, adhere to mat and vellum.

Glitzy Glitter

You have learned to love the self-adhesive nature of Magic Mesh. Now ask glitter to join the party! With a fingertip, simply dab a bit down on the mesh and it'll do the rest. Ultra fine glitter works the best for this.

Emboss It! With Heat or Dry

Like the weave but want it to match an item perfectly? No problem. Magic Mesh is very heat tolerant. You can heat emboss it with your favorite embossing powder color. Simply dab with embossing pad and sprinkle powder on it. Heat as you would with a heat tool until it melts to the perfect shade right before your eyes! You may even wish to embed your mesh in a thick layer of translucent embossing color. Give it a try!

To dry emboss, place your paper over the extra wide weave and apply pressure around the inside of the squares to raise the opposing side.

By snipping out a few corners you can make the squares as big as you like. These cut templates are reusable.

Blake's Zoo
by Jeannette Goyke

Little people love the zoo. But touching those animals is something else altogether.

MATERIALS: *Magic Mesh* Black fine • *DMD* (Tan, Brown cardstock, Light Brown vellum) • 1½" Brown die-cut letters • 22" Hemp • Gold mini brads • Pine needles • Black pen • Acid-free adhesive
INSTRUCTIONS:
Mat 2 photos on 1 Brown mat. Journal on a 3½" square piece of vellum. Cut an animal head from a photo. Frame a 3" wide x 10¾" piece of mesh with ⅝" strips of Brown cardstock. Adhere 'Blake's ZOO' to framed mesh so it reads through. Scatter pine needles through and under mesh and letters. Attach at bottom of page. Arrange elements. Wrap hemp around brads at all corners of the vellum. Loop hemp tail around the animal cutout, knot leaving 2" ends.

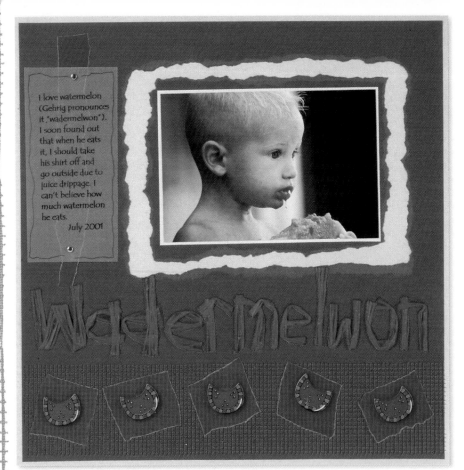

Wadermelwon
by Kelly Anglin

Get off that shirt and grab the camera!

MATERIALS: *Magic Mesh* Red fine • Paper (Hunter Green, Ecru, White) • *DMD* vellum (Red, Light Green) • *Paper Adventures* Red raffia • *Provo craft* watermelon wood embellishments • 2 Mini brads • Acid-free adhesive

INSTRUCTIONS:
Tear a 5½" x 7¾" window in upper half of Hunter Green paper. Mat the Green with Ecru. Make the window piece smaller, center this in hole as a mat for the photo. Mat photo with White paper, then glue to Green. Adhere a 2½" strip of mesh across bottom of page. Tear five 1½" to 2" squares of Red vellum. Space evenly on mesh, glue a watermelon piece on each. Write 'Wadermelwon' with raffia above mesh. Journal on Light Green vellum. Cut text to fit beside photo. Tear a strip of Red vellum longer than the Green. Fasten words over Red strip with 2 mini brads.

The journaling on the photo reads:
I love watermelon (Gehrig pronounces it "wadermelwon"). I soon found out that when he eats it, I should take his shirt off and go outside due to juice drippage. I can't believe how much watermelon he eats.
July 2001

Don't Let the Color Fool You!

Magic Mesh is a translucent material and the color will change to reflect whatever it is placed on. Notice how orange changes hues. Experiment yourself. Mix and match interesting shades from different spectrums to get that perfect blend.

Love Is
by Jeannette Goyke

The unconditional love your animals show you is priceless.

MATERIALS: *Magic Mesh* Red fine • *DMD* cardstock (Ecru, Black, Red) • Red chalk • *Sizzix* machine and 1½" dies (alpha, heart) • Black fine point pen • Acid-free adhesive

INSTRUCTIONS:
Tear a 2" strip from the top third of Ecru cardstock. Adhere mesh to Black cardstock where missing strip would be. Mat Ecru on Black. Cut a piece of Ecru narrower but longer than 1 photo, tear bottom edge. Glue photo to Ecru, mat with Red. Print 2 sets of words on Ecru. Tear edges of both. Rub chalk on Ecru edges at mesh, piece under photo and smaller word piece. Mat larger word piece on cut Red cardstock. Mat 2nd photo on Red. Place on page. Die-cut 'Love' 'xx' and 2 hearts. Outline 'Love' with pen. Cut 3 small squares of mesh. Assemble page.

is snuggling with your dad on a Sunday morning.

Chris, Scraps and Sydney
February 1997

Giddy Up

California State Fair

Mr. Green Bookworm Tag
by Sarah Cox

Let this cute guy hide in your book.

MATERIALS: *Magic Mesh* Lime Green fine • 2⅜" x 4¾" Yellow tag • 10" Lime Green fibers • *Scrapbook 101*, Renae Lindgren caviar bead worm applique • Acid-free adhesive
INSTRUCTIONS:
Adhere worm to tag. Cut ⅞" x 4¾" strip of mesh, remove half of the horizontal threads. Cut 1" x 4¾" strip, remove half of the horizontal threads. Adhere both to one edge of tag, trim hole corner at an angle. Tie fibers through hole.

Bug House
by Sarah Cox

Create this simple bug and frog card.
MATERIALS: *Magic Mesh* Green fine
• *Colorbok* stickers
• *Petite Motifs* Light Green cardstock • Acid-free adhesive
INSTRUCTIONS: Cut cardstock 5" x 6". Cut one 1⅞" x 6" strip mesh, cut one 2" x 6" strip. Remove top 2 or 3 horizontal rows of the mesh. Adhere to bottom of card. Add stickers.

Giddy Up
by Cindy A. Harris

Every kid should take a pony ride. Be sure to catch it on film!

MATERIALS: *Magic Mesh* Tan medium • *Bazzill* cardstock (Tan, Brown, White) • *Karen Foster* horseshoe pattern paper • *Scrap Pagerz* 1⅝" lettering template • *Stamp Doctor* 4 Brown eyelets • Eyelet setter • *Making Memories* Brown twistel • Black pen • Acid-free adhesive
INSTRUCTIONS:
Tear a 3" strip from the middle of the Brown Paper. Adhere Brown to horseshoe with top and bottom edges matching. Mat top half of photo with Brown, mat all with Tan. Place on page. Set eyelets in Brown section on sides of page. Lace twistel through eyelets, tie in front. Write words on White paper, tear around them. Cut ten 1½" squares of mesh, adhere 5 angled across top, 5 across bottom of page. Glue words across mesh at bottom. Cut out 'Giddy Up', adhere at top over mesh.

Happy Spring
by Michelle Tardie

Delight someone with this cheery card.

MATERIALS: *Magic Mesh* (fine Green) • Blank Green card • *Paper Fever* (paper, alphabet letters, Black border sticker) • *Making Memories* tag • *PSX* alphabet stamps • *Karen Foster* bug stickers • 4" - 6" fiber • Acid-free adhesive

INSTRUCTIONS:
Glue Pink paper rectangle onto blank card front. Cut mesh the width of card. Remove half the horizontal threads from top of mesh. Trim a few vertical strands to be uneven. Stick mesh strip to bottom of Pink rectangle. Place dragonfly and snail stickers on card. Place border strip at bottom, over edge of snail. Add color to tag, if desired. Stamp 'happy' on tag, attach fiber to tag. Arrange 'spring' on card, glue tag in place.

Through a Printer!

A friend in Scotland gets credit for this idea. He took a sheet of mini Q, still on its release sheet and selected a picture from clip art. He printed on it as if it were paper. The result looked like a cross stitched work of art! This technique would work well for family titles with heirloom looks. How would you use it? Let your imagination run wild.

Display Those Favorites!

This idea came from my mom. Your pre album favorites can be displayed in full view using Magic Mesh on the refrigerator. Pick a mesh color, peel off the backing and add those photos. You have an instant scrapbook on the fridge!

Fringe It!!

To get a fringed look with Magic Mesh, simply unravel a bit by pulling some strands off. For an uneven look, trim irregularly before removing those strands.

Make Fringe on Mesh!

Wrap It Up!
by Michelle Tardie

A gift bag will be as easy as 1, 2, 3 with a little creativity and Magic Mesh. And if the recipient is creative, he will save the mesh to use on his next project!

MATERIALS: *Magic Mesh* Tan medium • *DMD* bag • *Kopp Design* (pattern paper, word card, flower cut outs) • *Making Memories* twistel • *Craft T* Rub-ons • Acid-free adhesive

INSTRUCTIONS:
Cover bag front with pattern paper. Add mesh. Apply Rub-ons over mesh. Assemble elements on bag.

TIP - Simple Bookmarks

Color code articles in books and magazines with Magic Mesh. I use Red to mark a hot idea and Blue if something is kind of cool. Green works well for garden ideas. Mesh markers don't fall out and never ruin a page when being removed. A small piece will serve to mark many pages.

A Kid's Party and a Parent's Dream

No mess, no fuss! Let the kids stick it everywhere. Kids will enjoy the feel of Magic Mesh. You'll enjoy the amount of time they"ll spend playing with small pieces around the house, and not a surface will be damaged!

Bug Box/Birthday Box
by Karan Smith

MATERIALS: *Magic Mesh* fine Blue • *Highsmith* small box with handle • *Colorbok* bug stickers

INSTRUCTIONS: Cut a hole on both sides of box using handle hole as a template. Place mesh, adhesive side out, over side holes from inside of box. Assemble box, seal across the top with mesh. Decorate with bug or birthday stickers.

Simple Birthday Tag

MATERIALS: *Magic Mesh* fine (Red, Yellow, Blue) • 3" x 6" White tag • 3" x 3½" White vellum • *Funky Fibers* Red fibers • Red pen • Acid-free adhesive

INSTRUCTIONS:
Cut 1¼" squares of mesh. Apply to card. Tie fiber through tag hole. Write a message on vellum, adhere over mesh.

Welcome Spring... the flowers that bloom and the birds that sing.

Enjoy the soft breeze as it floats on by... making the clouds dance across the blue in the bright rays sky. Bask warmth of the yellow sun... it's shining down upon everyone. Breathe deeply the scents of Lilac and Rose... envelope your senses with each blossom that grows. Explore with your soul the new path nature brings...

A journey through the beauty of God's marvelous blessings. Treasure the sights and around... Revel in the joy that you've found. power and the glory of love Spring from the Lord above. the sounds all peace and new Believe in the that is sent with the

Mommy 2003

the glorious colors of

Welcome Spring
by Valoree Albert

A lovely poem for a lovely little girl!

MATERIALS: *Magic Mesh* Dotti Ann polka dot (Periwinkle, Lime, Pink, Green) • Cardstock (Blue, Ivory, Black) • *Creative Imaginations* Sonnets letter stickers • *Artistic Wire* 24 gauge tinned copper • Poem • Acid-free adhesive

INSTRUCTIONS:
Print poem on Ivory cardstock, leaving spaces for mesh blocks and photo. Tear right edge of Ivory, adhere to Blue cardstock. Mat photo on Black. Cut mesh triangles and rectangles to make 2" squares of 2 colors each. Tear four 1¾" squares of vellum. Make 2 flowers and 2 butterflies from wire. Adhere mesh squares, vellum, wire forms and photo to page. Stick 'Welcome' at top of poem.

Magic Mesh under Vellum

For a nice soft background use vellum over your chosen color of Magic Mesh.

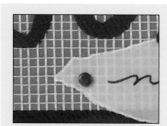

Secure vellum over mesh with eyelets or adhesive.

Simple Titles
by Cindy A. Harris

The simplest title becomes much more interesting with the addition of Magic Mesh.

MATERIALS: *Magic Mesh* White fine • Cardstock (Rust, Brown, Hunter Green) • *Sizzix* machine and 1¼" letter die-cuts • White vellum • 2 Mini brads • Black pen • Acid-free adhesive

INSTRUCTIONS:
Adhere mesh to Rust cardstock, cut title strip desired size. Cut Brown, tear one long edge. Mat Rust on Brown. Die-cut title letters from Hunter Green. Write 'nature' on vellum, tear around it. Attach vellum under title with brads.

Play Dress Up

From simple to simply awesome. Whether you're making a permanent outfit or removable clothes for a paper doll, Magic Mesh is the texture ticket!

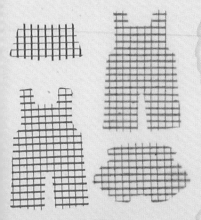

Cut or Die-cut clever clothing for paper dolls with colorful Mesh!

Create a unique mermaid with metallic mesh.

Mermaid Doll
by Marah Johnson

MATERIALS: *Magic Mesh* Copper fine • Tan cardstock • Blue, Green and Purple fibers • Metallic Rub-Ons (Green, Blue, Copper) • Pink chalk • Glue dots • Black pen or face stamp • 2 Brown mini brads • 1" of 24 gauge wire • *Suze Weinberg UTEE* • Heat gun • Seed beads • 5 E-beads • Thread • Acid-free adhesive

INSTRUCTIONS:
Draw a mermaid body on cardstock, draw arms separately with enough extra at top to hinge to the shoulders. Draw or stamp a face, cut to fit over head, glue in place. Use chalk to highlight cheeks. Make dot for navel. Punch hole in top of head, thread wire through hole, attach yarn. Secure yarn to back of head with glue dots. String E-beads in hair. Cut mesh top for doll, adhere. Color lower body and tail with Green and Blue Rub-Ons. Cover with UTEE, heat, repeat. Highlight tail with Rub-Ons again, heat. Attach mesh to hips and tail. Color mesh top, hip and tail with Copper Rub-On. String 3½" of beads, tie around neck. Attach arms to shoulders with mini brads.

Embellish Dolls with Wire and Mesh

Unique dolls like these call for unique materials. Be creative, use wire for arms and legs, Magic Mesh for clothes.

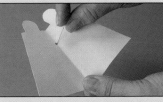

1. Punch a hole on the fold for arm wire.

2. Coil arm and leg wire around a thin rod.

3. Attach one end of each wire to inside of card.

Roadmap to my Heart Doll
by Marah Johnson

Give someone direction with this unique doll.

MATERIALS: *Magic Mesh* Red medium • *DMD* cardstock • *Sculpey* (clay, whimsical dolls push mold #APM25) • *PSX* roadmap stamp • *Pop Dots* • *Suze Weinberg* UTEE Bronze embossing enamel • 20 gauge Turquoise wire • 'Heart' bead • *Zucker* feathers • Craft glue

INSTRUCTIONS:
Mold clay feet and face, bake following manufacturer's directions. Cut cardstock large enough to double over to make doll body. Trace pattern, cut out. Stamp roadmap over the cardstock. On front, emboss using UTEE to adhere mesh to cardstock like roads. Stamp 'Roadmap to My' on cardstock, cut out letters. Place letters on pop dots. Arrange on doll. Place bead on pop dot, glue in place. Coil wire around a thin rod. Attach feet to leg wires, bend arm wires as if holding the signs. Glue wires and head in place. Glue feathers to back of head.

PATTERN FOR ROADMAP DOLL

Place on fold.

Blue Dream Doll   *by Marah Johnson*

MATERIALS: *Magic Mesh* fine (Grey, Silver) • *Bazzill* White cardstock • ¼" 'Dream' stamp • Blue ink pad • *Artistic Wire* Silver 24 gauge • *Funky Fibers* Blue fibers • 2 *Karen Foster* Silver star brads • 2" x 2" Slide mount • Silver foil • Assorted seed beads • *Craf-T* Rub-Ons (Turquoise, Pink, Purple) • *Suze Weinberg* UTEE • Heat gun • Black pen • Acid-free adhesive

INSTRUCTIONS:
Draw doll shape on cardstock, cover arm and leg areas with Grey mesh. Cut out doll. Cut arms, legs and head from body. Stamp or draw face. Tint cheeks with Pink, accent doll parts with Rub-Ons. Coat legs with UTEE, heat. Apply more Rub-Ons. Wrap wire around legs, ending with a coil on top of each foot. Cover slide mount with foil, apply Purple Rub-On to foil. Set star brads on top corners of mount. Stamp 'Dream' on cardstock, glue to opening in slide mount. Attach doll parts to mount. Accent word paper with Purple Rub-Ons. Cut Silver mesh larger than head, adhere to head. Attach hair to back of head and mesh. Thread 4 to 6 beads onto wire, bend end over and wrap to keep beads at ends. Attach to head like hair.

Circle of Love

Show someone you love them with this unique collage.

MATERIALS: *Magic Mesh* medium Red • Decorative papers (several patterns, Gold) • 1" Brass frame • CD • Cheesecloth • 'LOVE' stamp • Red ink pad • 20 Gauge Gold wire • Pink E beads • Heart charm • Red fibers • *Craf-T* Gold metallic Rub-Ons • *Suze Weinberg* UTEE • Heat gun • Tape • Glue stick • Acid-free adhesive

INSTRUCTIONS:

Trace CD onto decorative papers, cut out. Spread thin layer of glue on CD, attach papers. Cut 3 wide mesh pieces, adhere. Attach cheesecloth with glue stick. Highlight mesh and edges of CD with Rub-Ons. Layer with UTEE, heat. Stamp title on a strip of Gold paper, affix to CD, melt UTEE over it. String charm and beads onto wire. Wrap wire around ½ of CD with ornaments to front, attach to back. Wrap other half of CD with fiber, attach to back.

Spring Beauty

Dotti Ann and Magic Mesh reflect the wonderful colors of spring.

MATERIALS: *Magic Mesh* (Lavender fine, Lime Dotti Ann) • Design Originals Legacy Collage #0538 Violets Hanky paper• CD • Acetate sheet • Crystal flower embellishments.• *Artistic Wire* Gold 24 gauge • Light Green seed beads • *Suze Weinberg* UTEE • Heat gun • Acid-free adhesive

INSTRUCTIONS:

Tear papers, cut pieces of mesh, adhere to CD. Spread UTEE on outside and side edges, heat. Thread beads on wire, make loops and attach ends to back of CD. Glue embellishments in place. Print words on acetate, cut apart. Attach to CD.

Explore

Magic Mesh gives you little windows to peek through to explore the layers of design on this tin.

MATERIALS: *Magic Mesh* fine (Gold, Copper) • CD tin • *Design Originals* Legacy Collage Paper (# 0547 Dictionary) • Mulberry paper (Green, Olive Green) • Mica chips • Picture pebble • Charms • *US ArtQuest* Perfect Paper Adhesive • *Brilliance* Gold ink • *Suze Weinberg* UTEE • Heat gun • *Craf-t* Copper Metallic Rub-On • 3 Quotes • Fine sandpaper • Acid-free adhesive

INSTRUCTIONS:

Sand tin well to remove all gloss from finished surface, wipe clean. Tear pieces of dictionary paper, arrange, glue to tin. Coat with adhesive. Cut several pieces of Gold and 1 of Copper mesh, adhere to top of tin. Tear mulberry paper in small pieces, glue over mesh. Print or write in Green 3 quotes. Ink edges of tin with Gold, layer with UTEE, heat. Apply Copper Metallic Rub-On over UTEE covered edges, heat. Embellish with mica chips, picture pebbles and charms.

Chocolate Covered Strawberries
by Kimberly Sigler

MATERIALS: *Magic Mesh* (Red medium, Tan fine) • *Bazzill* cardstock (White, Red, Green, Brown) • Die-cut strawberries • Black pen • Acid free adhesive

INSTRUCTIONS:
Adhere 2½" x 2¾" squares of Tan mesh to corners of White cardstock. Cut two 2½" x 2¾" squares of Red mesh, cut on diagonal. Adhere Red mesh to Tan on corners. Print title, trim and mat with Red cardstock. Die-cut strawberries and leaf, cut chocolate from Brown cardstock. Assemble. Apply 1¼" strip of Red and 3" strip of Tan across center of page. Cut two 2½" strips of White cardstock, tear 1 long edge. Assemble page.

Love is...
Chocolate Covered Strawberries

... especially when they are buried in ice cream!

Time to Say Hi Tag
by Marah Johnson

MATERIALS: *Magic Mesh* Pink fine • White cardstock • *Design Originals* Legacy Collage papers (#0528 Watches; #0527 Pink Diamonds; #0541 Report Card) • Glass marble • Alpha rubber stamp • Black ink pad • Pink Rub-Ons • Acid-free adhesive

INSTRUCTIONS:
Cut cardstock to desired size, fold to make card. Cover card with decorative paper. Adhere mesh to top of card, apply Rub-Ons. Add decorative papers over mesh. Adhere mesh triangle to bottom of card. Stamp motto. Apply marble.

Thanks Tag
by Marah Johnson

MATERIALS: *Magic Mesh* Gold fine • *Design Originals* Legacy papers (#0495 Brown floral; #0498 TeaDye Tapestry) • 3" x 4¾" Tag • *Amaco* Copper Art-Emboss; Copper Wireform mesh • Flower punch • 'Thanks' rubber stamp • Brown ink pad • Gold metallic Rub-Ons • Brown mini brads • 8" Sheer ribbon • Acid-free adhesive

INSTRUCTIONS:
Glue Tapestry paper to tag. Cover with Gold mesh, apply Rub-Ons. Cover top and bottom of tag with Brown floral paper. Adhere mesh around tag hole. Insert ribbon, apply copper mesh and metal die-cut to tag. Stamp Ecru paper, apply to card with brads.

time to

say hi

Collage with Mesh

Subtle color changes and see-through mesh will add to the mystery of your creation. Let them hunt, make them wonder. Add layers of intrigue to your next project.

1. Cover item with decorative paper using an adhesive.

2. Tear or cut additional papers.

3. Adhere papers and mesh to surface.

4. Trim mesh if necessary. Add embellishments.

Collage with Mesh

Magic Mesh lends itself beautifully to collage. It provides texture, you can see through it, it creates subtle color variations and it is forgiving! You can create layers of design with mesh and just peel it off if you want to reposition it. Magic Mesh is a dream come true!

Thanks!

Little Things

Decorative designs from the past blend perfectly with the copper elements applied here. These pages join past and present with simple forms and related colors.

Happiness Book Cover

The front cover, made from old fabric, newsprint and nostalgic embellishments, conceals the visual excitement inside. Anything goes!

Timeless Beauty

Classic beauty will always be in good taste. Gather objects that complement the era. Old gauze, buttons that remind us of Grandma, bangles and beads. Subtle colors tame the explosion of texture on these pages.

Basic Materials

Magic Mesh • Board book • Cardstock • Papers • Paper souvenirs • Fabric • Ribbon • Acetate sheets • Sewing pattern pieces • Images • Wire • Safety pins • Tags • Brads • Rubber stamps • Ink pads • Acrylic paint • Gel medium • UTEE • Heat gun • Beads • Buttons • Slide mounts • Foils • Embellishments • Acid-free adhesive

A Pocket Full of Memorabilia

Create a pocket, fill it with memories. Gold and beads adorn this one. Anything can be used to make your pages interesting. Is this the pattern for the dress she wore that night?

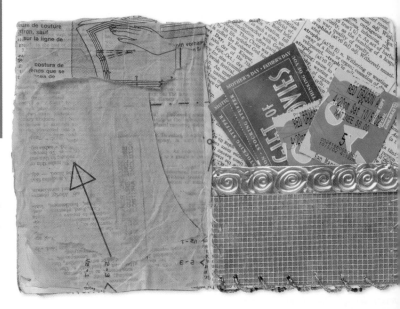

Postcard from the Past

Screen porches and fancy gloves. Who was he, anyway? Create mystery with tags and postal stamps. And always remember the interest you can create with texture.

Catch the Craze!

Altered books offer amazing possibilities. You can express a world of emotion in the pages of your own special book. Magic Mesh is a great tool to help unify objects, add texture and create depth. Gather the elements and create one soon!

Made by Hand

Remember the Red dress that Mother made you? She taught you to sew a button on that day. Recall the good times when people made memories with their own two hands.

Back Cover

Like the front, the subtle colors here only tempt you to look inside. Use interesting text to further intrigue those who pick up your book.

Pink Mango Delight

Be silly with a friend on a wild Pink afternoon. Sparkling butterflies and bright shiny beads complement your favorite smile. And never be afraid to giggle out loud!

Karan Smith

When she's not busy playing and wrestling her two boys, Parker, 6, Reece, 3, and husband Bryan, Karan finds herself dreaming up the unusual, in hopes of inspiring creativity in those touched by her product, Magic Mesh. It's no wonder this feisty redhead is always grinning.

Karan's biggest reward to date is having traveled to England and Scotland, seeing first hand the universal appeal of Magic Mesh.

After majoring in communications, she started her own magazine and enjoys writing. She is living proof of the "Do what you love" theory.

To order Magic Mesh supplies visit their website:

http://www.magicmesh.com
email: karan@magicmesh.com

phone 651-345-6374
fax 651-345-0120

Magic Mesh
PO Box 8,
Lake City, MN 55041

Magic Mesh adds color, texture, dimension and fun to pages!

MANY THANKS to my friends for their cheerful help and wonderful ideas!
Kathy McMillan • Jennifer Laughlin
Patty Williams • Marti Wyble
Janet Long • Barbara Worth
David & Donna Thomason

New Year's Eve was a chance for Gavin and I to kick up our heels! We were invited to a New Years Eve party at a waterfront restaurant on the Hawkesbury River, by some business friends. We had a lovely night chatting with the people on our table, and had a lovely meal, overlooking the boats below.

Easy, Neat Lettering Help!

1. Follow a chart for letters.

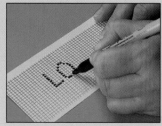

2. Use a marker to cross stitch or fill in squares.

If you're not one who likes the look of your own handwriting, make some neat straight styles using Magic Mesh as a grid.

Use a cross stitch chart to create letters and words that look great.

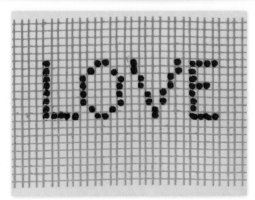

Remove Mesh from lettering or leave it in place.